GRIME AND PUNISHMENT

A Collection of Sexciting Puns

by HARVEY C. GORDON

Illustrations by Frank C. Coronado

Glancing Cheek to Cheek

WARNER BOOKS

A Warner Communications Company

Warner Books, Inc.,
75 Rockefeller Plaza,
New York, N. Y. 10019

Ⓦ A Warner Communications Company

Printed in the United States of America

First Printing: June 1981

10 9 8 7 6 5 4 3 2 1

LIBRARY OF CONGRESS CATALOGING IN PUBLICATION DATA

GORDON, HARVEY C   1947-
  GRIME AND PUNISHMENT.

  1. SEX—ANECDOTES, FACETIAE, SATIRE, ETC.
2. PUNS AND PUNNING. I. TITLE.
PN6231.S54G64   818'.5402   80-20987
ISBN 0-446-97026-3 (U.S.A.)
ISBN 0-446-97871-X (CANADA)

GRIME AND PUNISHMENT

Also by Harvey C. Gordon

PUNishment
The Art of Punning
or
How to Lose Friends and Agonize People

I dedicate this book
to my jock strap
for all the support
it has given me through the years

PREFACE

Shortly after the publication of my first book, *PUNishment—The Art of Punning or How to Lose Friends and Agonize People,* fellow punster Robert J. Herguth, a columnist for the Chicago *Sun-Times,* mentioned in what was then his Chicago *Daily News* column that since my book was relatively clean, I could not call it "Grime and PUNishment." Realizing the seriousness of this limitation, I started to develop some off-color material that could be used for a new book worthy of the title "Grime and PUNishment." What I came up with is a special collection of sexciting puns, which can be added to a punster's arsenal, affording him a new dimension for PUNishing his victims.

Since punning is a highly creative activity, *Grime and PUNishment* will do a great deal to develop and expand the art by tapping one of the greatest of all creative resources—the dirty mind. The book should stimulate a large number of potential punsters by exposing them to an enjoyable source of new material. People who might otherwise not be interested in punning will have a chance to appreciate puns because of the sexcitable nature of the book. Hopefully, even avowed abstainers will be enticed. By opening the door to an appealing source of new material and motivating readers to start using puns, *Grime and PUNishment* should go a long way toward achieving my goals of making punning a widespread art and having the art recognized as an important form of humor.

I have divided the puns in the book into two sections. The first contains my primary collection of sexciting puns, which should have a wide range of appeal. The second part consists of a smaller collection of the spiciest puns in the book, which I have called "X-citing."

Since Warner Books is an illustrious publisher, I decided to have a number of the puns in the book illustrated. However, because of my concern that off-color puns would result in off-color illustrations, I had all the drawings done in black and white. In creating the illustrations, my artist and I tried to em-barr-ass as few persons as possible.

In *PUNishment* I emphasized that what makes punning an art is the ability to blend puns smoothly into normal conversation and the knack of creating clever puns spontaneously in appropriate situations.* When present-

---

*See Appendix for a discussion of the punning techniques that can be used for blending puns smoothly into everyday conversation. The discussion consists of excerpts from PUNishment—The Art of Punning or How to Lose Friends and Agonize People, 2nd ed. (New York: Warner Books, 1980), Chapter 23, "Techniques for Punsters," pp. 107–120.

ing off-color puns at opportune moments, a punster must be sure to keep his composure and strive to be an artist in spite of the high degree of sexcitement that can be aroused by the occasion.

It was not my intention in writing this book to be chauvinistic or condescending toward either sex. My goal was simply to come up with the best possible puns and use any format that would express them effectively.

I hope I have put sufficient grime in this book to compensate for the small degree of sexcitement in my first book. If, however, I have not succeeded in satisfying my readers—if *Grime and PUNishment* is still considered relatively clean—I shall feel immorally obligated to do a book of hardcore punography that would have to be called *Slime and PUNishment.*

CONTENTS

SEXCITING PUNS

After winning the league championship, a seven-foot basketball player walked into his favorite bar and said, "The highballs are on me."

Many women do not enjoy having a basketball player for a lover. They always dribble before they shoot.

I heard about a high-priced call girl staying at a classy hotel in New York who charges one thousand dollars a night for her services. The hotel refers to her suite as "The Grand Ballroom."

A woman had a breast enlargement operation and was delighted with the results. She wrote a special note to her doctor that read: "Thanks for the mammaries."

I know a guy who often fools around with his secretary at the office. When he does, he goes home and tells his wife he had a hard day at the office.

Upon hearing that his wife had given birth to quintuplets, a civil rights activist back in 1966 allegedly said, "I have overcome."

A number of normal, healthy babies have been conceived by artificial insemination, which tends to disprove the old saying: "Spare the rod and spoil the child."

A photographer interviewed a number of bathing beauties to pose for a men's magazine. Some of the girls were unsuited for the job.

During his evening security check, a bailiff entered the judge's chambers and unexpectedly found the judge making love to one of the court reporters. "Your Honor!" the startled bailiff exclaimed. "No, you fool," the annoyed judge replied, "she's on me."

After auditioning in a bikini for a part in a commercial, a voluptuous girl leaned over and told the man in charge, "If you're interested, you know where to get a hold of me."

A couple of women joined a strip poker game with a group of men and managed to raise them a number of times.

The police recently raided a massage parlor on the Near North Side of Chicago. Apparently, a masseuse rubbed someone the wrong way.

A few years ago a friend of mine picked up his date and told her they were going to see the movie *Papillon*—a film about a French penal colony. His date shyly inquired whether the movie was about an all-male nudist camp.

Shortly after arriving in Hollywood, an attractive young actress got involved in successive love affairs with two of the screen's leading actors. The woman had always had a desire to make love under the stars.

A call girl in Dallas was once entertaining a young cowboy from a small west Texas town and was quite impressed with the young man's sexual sophistication. "I see you're no stranger to these parts, sonny," the woman acknowledged.

Some men do not sleep well on their honeymoon. They get up three or four times a night.

I met a taxidermist in London who always takes a woman out for a big meal before making love to her. He's used to stuffing a bird before mounting her.

When told by his boss to start developing a robot that could engage in sexual intercourse, the engineer replied, "I'll get right on it."

A man who had had a few too many drinks loudly propositioned a woman in a crowded singles bar and was thrown out by the manager for engaging in aural sex. (When the man continued to harass the woman outside the bar, he was arrested and charged with disturbing the piece.)

Many farmer's daughters will only make it with city men because farm hands are too rough.

A man was confronted by his wife about his involvement with another woman and confessed to having a second marriage in another state. When his wife reacted with disbelief, the man said, "I think it was bigamy to admit it."

I understand that going out with a castrating female can be a eunuch experience.

An elderly gentleman was greatly concerned about being able to satisfy his lady friend during their first night together. Fortunately, he was able to rise to the occasion.

Upon arriving at his date's apartment for dinner, the insecure man proceeded to tell her a number of stories about his exploits as a great lover. Eventually, the woman said, "Now that we've had our cocktails, it's time for dinner."

A number of prostitutes are apathetic about voting in elections. They don't care who gets in.

A woman who likes to monkey around with lots of men might be described as an organ grinder.

During the Middle Ages a number of maidens sought comfort on long, lonely knights.

A college girl went to a fraternity beer party (I Phelta Thi Fraternity), got drunk, spent the night with one of the fraters, and soon after discovered that she was pregnant. After her baby was born, she decided to write a book about her experience, which she entitled *From Beer to Maternity*.

Two married women were out having lunch together. One of the women told her companion a dirty joke she had heard recently, and when her friend did not crack a smile, she said, "Don't you get it?" Her companion replied, "Not very often."

I heard about a salesman who sells padded bras from door to door. Women refer to him as the fuller bust man. (I understand that whenever he goes out selling, he wears his best duds.)

A couple came home from a New Year's Eve party shortly after midnight to make love. They wanted to start the new year off with a bang.

I understand that many chess players have love affairs in Czechoslovakia. They love Czech mates.

Did you hear about the successful porno movie that grossed several million?

When asked if she would take a personal check, the call girl replied, "I'll take a personal Czech, an impersonal Irishman, or anyone else who will pay the price."

One business executive we know allows his secretary to schedule all his appointments because he knows she's great on dates.

A number of younger men get religious during lovemaking. They often talk about the Second Coming.

An X-rated western is going to be released shortly. The wagons are the only things that will be covered.

Many lovemaking sessions end with a gland finale.

An actor and actress who have made a number of porno flicks are now out of work. You might say that they are among the hardcore unemployed.

Some women compare sex with a new partner to an impending winter storm; they don't know how many inches they will get nor how long it will last.

A couple was becoming quite frustrated over the man's prolonged period of impotency and decided to seek professional help. After three sessions of sexual therapy, the matter was brought to a head.

Some college girls have a faculty for making love; others just do it with fellow students.

A member of the faculty orientation committee was summoned to the Chancellor's office after allegedly fooling around with one of the freshman girls during orientation week. His defense was that he was just getting to know the student body.

When at first the aggressive coed could not convince her date to make love, she tried some genital persuasion.

A male Olympic swimming coach kept a shapely girl on the team even though she was not one of the best swimmers. Apparently, he liked her strokes.

I understand that a number of call girls have been recruit-ed by the CIA. They work as undercover agents.

A businessman phoned a call girl upon arriving in town and asked, "Are you free tonight?" "No," the woman replied, "but I'm reasonable."

There is a lady of the evening who follows the fleet to a number of European ports. When asked why she travels so much to entertain sailors, she replied, "I really go for semen."

I understand that prudent sailors will not make Waves.

A guy and his girlfriend were parked and "going to it" in the front seat of his car. In the heat of passion (and much to his embarrassment), the eager lover repeatedly hit the steering wheel horn with his body. After several honks, the girl finally said, "I didn't realize you were so horny."

When a college man told his girlfriend that the time was right for them to make love, she replied, "I'm with you every inch of the way."

A social-climbing American woman took advantage of her trip to Europe to meet and pursue some of the continent's most prominent noblemen. She managed to make every second count.

I used to go out with a girl whose kissing left something to be desired—the rest of her body.

A cheerleader for a professional football team lost her job after she appeared in a pornographic movie. She'll now have to find a new position.

Many women will not date a defensive lineman on a football team; all they have on their mind is sacks.

A lady invited a gentleman over to her house for dinner and a moonlight skinny dip in her private pool. To set the mood, the lady served strip steaks for dinner.

A call girl once told a friend about a well-endowed man who always paid her with silver dollars. She referred to him as "Long John Silver."

A woman was romantically involved with her dentist and planning to stay overnight at his apartment. She told him not to forget to cap it before he proceeded with the inlay.

Many girls who work in brothels eventually take up long-distance jogging. They're used to one lap after another.

An aspiring young actress decided to have silicone implants and a rear-end lift after she was told by a Broadway producer that before she could become a star she would have to become a little meteor.

After reviewing some of her film clips, a director decided not to hire a former porno star for a leading role in a new movie. Apparently, he did not like her parts.

When a world-renowned bridge player was asked what he would do if he held the queen alone, he replied, "Take her to bed until the king was expected home."

I heard about a call girl who keeps a diary of all her experiences. She once made an entry about an eighty-year-old patron that read: "He's the oldest trick in the book...."

There is a sheik in the Middle East who has nine wives. Eight of them have it pretty soft.

A teller at a local bank who enjoys flirting with the bank's customers recently became pregnant. Apparently, someone made a very special deposit.

In recent years there has been a tremendous surge in the number of women who have taken up jogging. The figures are fantastic.

A woman who was out to dinner with her husband, Tex, dropped her coat while walking out of the restaurant and said, "Please pick up my coat, Sam." Once they were in the car, her husband asked why she had called him "Sam" in the restaurant. The woman replied, "I was too embarrassed to say, 'Pick up my coat, Tex.' "

Scientists can always tell if a chromosome is male or female by taking off its genes.

A young married couple decided to seek counseling about their deteriorating sex life, which was attributable to their mutual desire to be on top during lovemaking. They told the therapist that the problem was mounting.

With the Russian invasion of Afghanistan, a number of lines from the sixties are being revived, such as: "Brezhnev pull out—like your father should have."

A playboy fashion designer, pretending to be interested in the fabric an attractive model was wearing, pinched some material from the upper portion of her dress and said, "Can this be felt?"

Fewer and fewer women feel comfortable going to the Virgin Islands for their wedding night.

A survey has disclosed that a high proportion of the couples that engage in wife-swapping are golfers. They're real swingers.

Golfers have been known to work on their putting game after the sun goes down. In fact, a fellow once told me he made a five-footer under the moonlight.

A woman brought a paternity suit against her psychologist. Apparently, when sex was discussed during their therapy sessions, the woman was quite open.

Ten minutes after finishing her sentence for prostitution, a hooker unknowingly solicited an undercover policeman on the street and was taken back into custody. Her second arrest illustrates the rule that one should never end a sentence with a proposition.

A husband and wife and their respective attorneys were trying to work out a mutually acceptable divorce settlement. At one point the exchange became quite emotional when the husband said to his wife, "We upped our offer. Up yours."

When I was in Hawaii, I saw a beautiful display of hula dancing; you might say that hula dancing is an asset to Hawaiian music.

A farmer's daughter who attends the State Fair for the first time will get herself in a lot of trouble if she cannot keep her calves together.

The atmosphere at a nudist colony is very relaxed. The members let it all hang out.

A man went into a bank to purchase a Certificate of Deposit and hit it off with the new accounts lady. After going out a few times and becoming physically involved, the lady decided to end the relationship. When the man asked why she was breaking things off, she replied, "As I told you at the bank, early withdrawal results in loss of interest."

I understand that the person who created the miniskirt was a sex enthusiast named Seymour Butz. (I wonder what he's up to now.)

A well-endowed woman who could only support herself by working as a topless dancer was once chastised about her profession. "Well," she replied sadly, "it's better than being flat busted."

Men who go out hunting at singles bars like to find women who are game.

A female singles tennis star from the United States got herself pregnant while on tour in Europe. She is now playing doubles.

At Wimbledon this year one of the female tennis players popped out of the top of her dress while trying to return a low shot. You might say she had a falling out with the crowd.

An attractive girl from the Midwest wanted to be an actress more than anything. She moved to New York, enrolled in acting school, and then made her way into show business.

I heard about a prudish female elevator operator who was fired from her job because she refused to tell riders that she was going down.

A hotel with deluxe banquet facilities caused a number of auto mishaps in an affluent California community when it put up a roadside sign that read: "Have Your Next Affair Here."

For a swinging playboy businessman, business is always picking up.

A man and a woman who were having an ongoing love affair had different lovemaking preferences. He enjoyed wild and passionate sessions, while she preferred slow and gentle intimacy. After dinner at a restaurant one night, the man said to his lady, "My pace or yours?"

I know a man who was married to a woman named Edith and having a glorious affair with a young girl named Kate. His wife found out about the affair and divorced him immediately, which only goes to show you that you can't have your Kate and Edith too.

When I was in Maui, I visited a crowded nude beach where everyone was glancing cheek to cheek.

The nude beach was separated from the main beach by a small cliff; a sign was posted at the entrance that read: "Please bare with us." Once at the nude beach, I soon realized how nervous I was when I walked up to a lady to get change for a phone call and asked if she had two nipples for a dime.

The brassiere industry has really gone to the dogs. The new bras are turning setters into pointers.

A nudist colony usually has a number of sunbathing buffs.

Instead of walking around and showing off at a nude beach, a woman with a great body will often lay face down in the sand to make a good impression.

A couple of nudists who were dating each other exclusively for about six months recently decided to go out with other people. They felt they were seeing too much of each other.

After seeing a veteran water skier take a hard fall during a water show, a female newspaper reporter asked him whether anything was worn under his bathing suit. The water skier replied, "No, ma'am. Everything's as good as it ever was."

A high school freshman invited some of his boyfriends over to watch a stag film that his older brother had rented in honor of his fifteenth birthday. By the end of the film, there wasn't a dry fly in the house.

Many international playboys have been recruited into our diplomatic service. They're well versed in foreign affairs.

A businesswoman in a low-cut dress attended a meeting with a number of men and felt very insecure. It seemed that everyone was looking down on her.

Some male bosses will not hire a secretary or receptionist until they have checked out her legs. Other bosses are above that.

The luckiest hours for men in Paris are between midnight and 4:00 A.M., and are known as "the oui hours of the morning."

A number of playboys should try out for our Olympic swimming team since they excel in the breast stroke.

Have you heard about the young lovers who didn't fall asleep until after three?

A Vietnam veteran decided to write a book about his combat experiences and the nights he spent with the ladies of the evening in Saigon. His book is entitled *War and Piece.*

A young actor was advised by his agent to model nude for a women's magazine. The agent apparently felt his client needed the exposure.

A cheerleader for a college football team decided to have a breast enlargement operation shortly before the first football game. It was the first two-point conversion of the season.

I was told about a female cheerleader for the University of Minnesota football team who had a lot of school spirit. She would gopher any player on the team.

A recent survey of coeds disclosed that football players who play split end and flanker back are the least desirable lovers on campus. Apparently, no girl wants you when you're down and out.

Two college girls arrived back at the dormitory late on a Saturday night and were interrogated by the dorm supervisor. "Why were you out after hours?" the woman asked. "Because we met two guys who were after ours," the girls replied.

Did you hear about the man on the flying trapeze who caught his wife in the act?

I know a secretary who has been pregnant so many times that whenever she types a letter, she automatically skips two consecutive periods.

A businessman first told his secretary to buy herself a new dress for her birthday. Then, he tried to talk her out of it.

Some law firms are going to extreme measures to win cases. One firm had birth control pills clandestinely placed in all the opposing firm's copying machines so they wouldn't reproduce.

Some lawyers who go out to court end up without their briefs.

A woman ran into a man she knew at the theater and unknowingly introduced him to a girlfriend who had once been his lover. The man said, "I think I've already made your acquaintance."

When a newly married woman told her girlfriend that married life was a pain in the ass, her girlfriend replied, "You're doing it all wrong."

A high school senior thought he had enough time to make love to his girlfriend in his room while his mother was making dinner. When his mother called him to eat sooner than expected, the boy yelled, "I'm coming!"

There is an attractive coed at the local university with measurements of 36-23-36 who has the reputation of being a complete prude. When men pass her on campus, they shake their heads and say, "What a waist."

A bachelor friend of mine was once telling me about one of his many loves. "I used to kiss her lips," he said, "but it's all over now."

I know a bachelor who has a very liberal outlook on life; you might say he's very broad-minded.

One night last year a couple made love in the heat of passion and forgot to take any birth control precautions. They now consider their baby a bungle of joy.

A New York writer was offered an excellent opportunity to go to Hollywood and write for a popular TV show. However, the voluptuous woman he was living with did not want to move to the West Coast. For the writer, it was clearly a case of Hollywood or bust.

I guess you've heard about the unfortunate Japanese call girl; no one had a yen for her.

A young lady was very frustrated because nothing was happening in her love life. She was truly fit to be tried.

Men who make obscene phone calls have sexual hangups.

A roller skate manufacturer and an athletic supporter company recently decided to merge because they both were familiar with ball-bearing items.

Most prostitutes do not care about a customer's name. They think of him as John Dough.

Gigolos achieve success in an unconventional way. They start on top and work their way down.

A man and a woman met each other while sitting at a bar. After a while the man said, "If I have one more drink, I'll start to feel it," to which the woman replied, "If I have one more, I'll let you."

I know a chauffeur who played strip poker last night for the first time. He learned that the more you lose, the more you have to show for it.

A famous Las Vegas hotel has a special suite for a well-endowed female entertainer who often performs at the hotel's nightclub. The suite has no doorbell—just two knockers.

An American college student on a tour of Finland was able to use his limited Finnish vocabulary to persuade a pretty native girl to spend the night with him. Upon departing for Sweden the next morning, the man apologized for his lack of familiarity with the girl's language by saying, "I'm afraid my Finnish isn't too good," to which the girl responded, "Neither is your foreplay."

A smooth-talking ladies' man who was hitchhiking through the French countryside was able to persuade a number of country girls to join him in the hayloft. You might say that the man is for whom the belles roll.

There is a bachelor principal at the local high school who has a reputation for being a great lover. The women teachers refer to him as "the peter principal."

A friend of mine told me he reads *Playboy* and *Penthouse* for the same reason he reads *National Geographic*—to see beautiful places he will never visit.

I heard about an elderly gentleman who went to bed with a lady friend at two in the afternoon and didn't get up until five.

A friend of mine told me that on his last trip to Paris he met and became friendly with an attractive French girl. The first night he made love to her in his hotel room he recalls her saying "Je t'adore" over and over, and he kept replying, "It's closed, it's closed."

Members of a college fraternity built a raft and floated down the local river with their rear ends exposed. Allegedly, the incident was the inspiration for the song "Moon River."

A middle-aged man who was depressed because he was aging had a number of one-night stands with younger women; however, each affair only added to his severe depression. You might say the man was falling apart piece by piece.

Apparently, some ladies of the evening make less than the minimum wage. I overhead one woman say that on a good night she can make two bucks an hour.

A well-known Caribbean resort recently became a nudist retreat and the resort's apparel shop decided to have a clothes-out sale.

A visit to a nudist camp can be very therapeutic for a marriage. It's a good place for a couple to air their differences.

The interiors of some drive-in movies are quite plush. They have wall-to-wall car petting.

A number of drive-ins are fully automated—during the movie.

An old maid might be considered a woman who has not met her maker.

I understand that most prostitutes calculate their annual income on December 31st. It's the end of their physical year.

A lady saw her bachelor neighbor enter his apartment with an intoxicated woman on his arm. The next day she saw him in the hall and said with a smile, "Who was that girl I saw you outwit last night?"

When the nightclub comedian had a few drinks and did a striptease on stage, the audience had a chance to watch a comic strip.

A dentist was accused of taking sexual liberties with one of his patients while she was under sedation. When the woman's attorney requested access to her dental file, he was told that it could not be found. The attorney replied, "The file isn't the only thing that's been mislaid."

Sometimes life for a prostitute can be a real grind.

A girl was somewhat disappointed with her first sexual experience. She told one of her friends, "It was no big thing."

Some high school teachers have affairs with their fellow faculty members while others stick to their principals.

A mixed doubles team at a singles resort did not hit it off well either on or off the court because he wanted to score and she wanted to end up with love.

There is a room in a Nevada brothel that is occupied by an enthusiastic, heavyset girl who has caused painful experiences for many of her customers. The room is often referred to as "The Nutcracker Suite."

A middle-aged man whose marriage revolves around the kitchen and the bedroom is unhappy because in one place it's always well done and in the other place it's rare.

The lecherous senior partner of a law firm told the attractive newly hired female attorney the following: "In order to get ahead in this firm and make it big, you'll have to practice for a while and get some experience under your belt."

I knew a girl in high school who was as pure as Snow White; however, she has since drifted quite a bit.

A coed and her boyfriend from the state university decided to check into a motel for the five days between their winter and spring courses. You might describe this part of their curriculum as "intercourse."

A former Miss America was running for national office. In discussing her successful fund raising, a newscaster said, "She has quite a campaign chest."

I heard about a prostitute who has a strong preference for chubby men; apparently, she believes in living off the fat of the land.

A novelty company is coming out with his-and-hers candy underwear. The female version is plain while the male version comes with nuts.

At a singles bar (unlike in a football game) a field goal kicker can score with a near miss.

I heard about a local organization that arranges call girls in different cities for traveling businessmen. They call the arrangement their layaway plan.

Many traveling businessmen take unfair advantage of their hotel accommodations. Some put towels in their suitcase; others get a maid in their grip.

A man and his wife were sunbathing at the French Riviera and observing sunbathers of the opposite sex. When an attractive French girl walked by in a topless bathing suit, the wife noticed that her husband looked longer.

Most bisexuals do not have strong political convictions. When it comes to voter referendums, they can go either way.

A photographer once brought his attractive assistant into the darkroom for half an hour to see what would develop.

Did you hear about the overly anxious baseball player who went for a fast ball, popped up, and could not score?

A man and a woman met at a tennis club and decided to rally for a while. As they approached the court, the man asked, "Is that a new can?" The woman looked down over her shoulder and replied, "No; it's the same one I've always had."

When a jockey picks up a girl who's hot to trot, he'll take her to a hotel and check into the Bridal Suite. (Some jockeys have a one-track mind.)

Lady Godiva was the biggest gambler of all time. She put everything she had on a horse. (While she didn't win, she showed all the way.)

A woman entertained a lover while her husband was working late, and was not careful about protecting her bedsheets. When her husband was getting into bed that night, she smiled at him but he looked at her with disdain.

A high school guy spent the weekend at his girlfriend's house while her parents were out of town. When her parents unexpectedly walked in on them, they were in a state of shack.

When told about a woman living near the base who took on twenty-five men in one night, the private from Alabama said, "Twenty-five! That's a lot of sheet!"

A female English lawyer will have trouble getting a job with an American law firm if she has worked as a solicitor.

The perfect day for a male attorney is lots of fee mail in the morning and a lot of female in the evening.

A topless dancer was told by her boss that she would get twice as much money if she danced bottomless and there were no strings attached.

American Indians do not say the word "How" anymore because they already know how; they just want the opportunity.

A young lady only streaked topless across campus because a completely nude body was more than she could bare.

An enterprising hooker bought a bicycle and peddled it all over town.

A man who believed that he would require a sex change operation to become a happy, fulfilled person decided to first get some psychiatric help. When the psychiatrist persuaded him that a sex change was not necessary to solve his problems, the man said, "That's a load off my chest."

To a playboy the expression "knock on wood" means banging on a wooden floor.

A man decided to ask the baker's shapely assistant out because he liked her buns.

The most effective oral contraceptive for a woman is the word "No."

A prudent bachelor will always carry contraceptives with him so they will be available on every conceivable occasion.

There was an attractive coed at the school I attended who was most accommodating to the guys in my fraternity. Her name was "June," but everyone called her "May."

A couple went to a therapist about a sexual problem involving the husband's dislike for the dominant position during intercourse. Eventually, the wife and therapist agreed that the problem was "Sir Mountable."

In the business world, an aggressive woman who will not take things lying down could end up in the top position.

A female espionage agent tried to seduce a man to get valuable information without knowing that the man was impotent. It turned out to be emission impossible.

Initially, the teen-aged girl was able to keep her pregnancy a secret from her friends; however, months later her situation became apparent.

A man on a business trip went to a singles bar, approached two ladies, and offered either of them fifty dollars to spend the night with him. One girl stormed out in a rage, but the other remained cool, calm—and collected.

I know a woman who has a foot fetish. She only makes it with well-endowed men.

My cousin knows a woman who has lived with four different men over the past five years. You could describe her as a busybody.

A judge's wife told her husband that his preoccupation with work was ruining their sex life. He was just going through the motions.

After having the same two prostitutes brought before him for the third time, the irritated judge said, "You ladies are not getting the point even though it has been pounded into you over and over."

Two American law students were touring a museum in London and walked by a medieval chastity belt. One student said to the other, "That must have been the very first antitrust suit."

Have you heard about the middle-aged lovers who were too tired to stay awake for a second?

Smoking pot and making love have one basic similarity—they're both joint ventures.

A man walked into his doctor's office and said to the shapely receptionist, "If I told you that you had a great body, would you hold it against me?"

The schoolmarm invited an Italian gentleman to her house for dinner. When she asked him what he wanted for dessert, the man put his arm around her and said, "Marmalade."

A man brought a one-million-dollar personal injury suit against his ex-wife for allegedly causing him to become impotent. However, his cause of action was unsuccessful. The evidence did not stand up in court.

There is an artist who specializes in obscene oil portraits. His paint is made from crude oil.

Some women get married for strange reasons. I know a lady who got married because her slip was showing.

A receptionist was excited about the opportunities at her new job. Her boss told her there would be many chances for advances.

I heard about a woman who has been involved with a number of players on the New York Jets. Her breasts are now referred to as "The Jet Set."

A woman who is anxious to conceive and imagines the symptoms of a pregnancy that has not occurred is laboring under a misconception. (She also has preconceived notions about parenthood.)

When a thirty-three-year-old woman told her gynecologist that she and her husband were ready to start a family, the gynecologist told her, "You had better get on the stick."

A male and female optometrist who share the same office suite were grinding away together in the office one day and made a spectacle of themselves.

I heard about a high-priced call girl who called all her customers "John" for short because she never knew anyone too long.

A high school boy brought his girlfriend and sleeping bag to a secluded spot at an outdoor concert with great expectations. However, the musicians produced the only score of the evening.

When at first the unpassionate playboy was unable to seduce his date, he tried a little ardor.

A house where a family with nine children resides could be a house of Pill refute.

At the office Christmas party everyone was feeling merry, so she left.

For female employees, wild Christmas parties can become an ass-felt jungle.

There is a company executive who cheats on his wife, drinks heavily, and is a compulsive gambler. His associates unofficially refer to him as "the Vice President."

Sometimes looks can be deceiving. An Englishman once told me he met a girl who appeared to be as pure as gold, but turned out to be a common (wh)ore.

There is a Nevada house of prostitution with a sign by its front door that reads: "Give our staff a chance to satisfy yours."

A well-endowed lady who was speaking on the Dean Martin Celebrity Roast was flanked by two male TV stars. She said, "Who ever thought I would be standing here with two biggies."

The publisher of a horse-breeding magazine with declining circulation is planning to feature a topless woman on one of its prime young horses every month. This feature will be advertised as their monthly center foal. (The publisher hopes it will stirrup some interest in the magazine.)

A modest woman who was vacationing at a dude ranch in Arizona was shocked when the riding instructor asked her if she wanted to ride bare back.

Right before his wedding the groom's father took his son aside and said, "Son, I want to give you some advice about sex and real estate and the advice is the same: Get lots while you're young!"

A smooth-talking playboy persuaded a young lady to take him back to her apartment and then tried to impress her with a philosophical discussion of the hereafter. After a short while, the man began to loosen his tie and said, "Speaking of the hereafter, let me show you what I'm here after."

I understand that a "condominium" is nothing more than a prophylactic for a small person.

I heard about a French lady on tour of the national zoo in Washington who ran into the ladies' room when she saw a sign at one of the exhibits that read: "Zebra Is Now on Display."

A businessman who liked to pat his female employees on the fanny was warned by the women that they would file a sexual harassment complaint if he touched them again, and there were to be no ifs, ands, or butts.

I would have to say that when it comes to women, my friend Louie is a connoisseur. He shacked up with two beautiful women for the weekend and is now "kinda sore" from it.

A short man asked a tall well-endowed model to dance without knowing that she was married to a boxer. The man got busted in the mouth.

More and more women can only resist temptation once weakly.

A California surfer parked his van at the beach, took his girlfriend in back, and then drove it home.

A Canadian woman told her eighteen-year-old daughter to see a doctor about birth control if she was planning to become sexually active. "Remember," the woman said with a smile, "as the French say here in Quebec, 'One egg is an oeuf.' "

A man does not need a financial adviser to know that sex is not a good investment. He won't get out of it what he puts into it.

I heard rumors that a girdle company and an athletic supporter company will be the new co-sponsors of the TV program *Meet the Press.* They want to change the program's name to *Press the Meat.*

An elderly Jewish man had a call girl in his London hotel room and inadvertently left his English money in his trousers when he went to the washroom. The woman grabbed the trousers and ran out the door with the man yelling, "My pence! My pence! Bring back my pence!"

When a streaker ran across the stage of *The Tonight Show,* the incident was reported in a news flash.

A woman who had been going out with a married man for six months is not sure where the relationship is going. She has been kept in the dark.

You might say that silicone injections are the answer to a maiden's pair.

A number of years ago a former college cheerleader did not try out for the Los Angeles Rams' cheerleading squad because she did not want to be an Embraceable Ewe.

A streaker once ran into a policewoman on the outskirts of the college campus; however, she was unable to pin anything on him.

I know a woman officer in the army who never takes her meals with the other officers. She likes to mess with the enlisted men.

I have been told that some WACs burn themselves out at an early age.

A couple of women decided to move from their apartment when the traffic signals at the surrounding intersections froze from the cold. They did not want to live in a red-light district.

The owner of a flower shop asked his shapely young assistant to stay late one night and help him inventory and rearrange all of the store's merchandise. When the man's wife dropped by the shop around ten, she caught her husband with his plants down.

A sorority planned to sell some home-baked goods on campus to raise money for charity. They put a sign in front of their house that read: ". . . We Deliver."

There is an obscene nightclub entertainer in Las Vegas who considers himself a band singer. His singing has been banned in a number of states.

A topless female band can have lots of sax appeal.

Two teen-aged boys who were out on a hot double date entered a drive-in movie in the middle of the picture. A couple of hours later the boys went to the men's room, and upon returning to the car, one remarked to the other, "This is where we came in."

A man who marries an old lady for money could be left holding the bag.

The increased amount of nudity in recent movies has appealed to film buffs.

A woman can always tell an old man in the dark. It isn't hard at all.

I hear there is a new book coming out entitled *The Alien Hooker*. It's supposed to be quite a horror story.

Many hookers believe in astrology. They read their horescope every day.

A bank examiner will pay special attention to a bank where many loans and unmarried female employees are overdue.

Bankers have a hard time understanding why a woman without principle will draw a lot of interest.

When her parents went out of town, a high school girl let her boyfriend spend the night with her; however, she would not admit it.

A number of magicians will hire former prostitutes as assistants. They already know how to do tricks.

Tiny prostitutes have a tendency to sell themselves short.

When a well-endowed country singer fainted on stage, it took six men to carry her off—three abreast.

A girl at one of the local high schools thought she was entitled to a varsity letter for making the basketball team.

A basketball player thinks of lovemaking with the woman on top as a lay-up.

The wealthy hermit who has not been with a woman in ten years considers himself to be a self-made man.

I understand they have made an X-rated movie sequel to the Cinderella story in which the Prince goes through a prolonged period of impotency, and Cinderella, after acting out a number of fantasies without success, wistfully sighs, "Someday my prince will come."

A shapely farm girl was selling apples at the State Fair when a young man approached her stand. "Sir, would you like to buy some of my apples?" "No," the man replied, "but I'm interested in your pair."

I heard rumors that a new hardcore porno movie is in the works. The producers would like to use the title *The Pit and the Pendulum.*

A boy from Boston was telling his high school friends about the "summer girls" he met at Cape Cod. "Some are for friendship and some are for fun," the boy said with a smile.

A nervous teenager forgot his contraceptives on the occasion of his first sexual experience. The resourceful youth used a thin stocking as a condom and socked it to her.

To satisfy some women, a professional stud will have to put in overtime. (Eventually, however, he will peter out.)

A playboy sea captain will always have an attractive first mate on board. (He will also have an attractive second, third, and fourth mate around.)

I read about an innkeeper's daughter during the Middle Ages who made love for fifteen straight knights.

In biblical times some enterprising prostitutes tried to make a prophet.

I understand that some women who have to walk alone at night attach mousetrap-type gadgets to their bras in case they are attacked. These innovative devices might be called "booby traps."

A female science teacher with a great figure was starting a unit on astronomy with her junior high class. After a brief introduction, she asked the class which part of the Universe interested them most. A boy in the front row promptly replied, "Uranus."

The money made from the sale of stag films might be described as gross profit.

A couple who was eager to have children had one of the woman's fertilized eggs implanted in a surrogate mother. You might say the couple believes in giving the united way.

Last night I went to a disco lounge and saw a disco exhibition by a well-endowed young woman. The dancer was quite outstanding.

A striptease dancer was doing her thing on stage when the theater curtains fell and completely engulfed her. The dancer threw off the curtains and yelled, "I've been draped."

To the men who watch them, striptease dancers are girls with appeal.

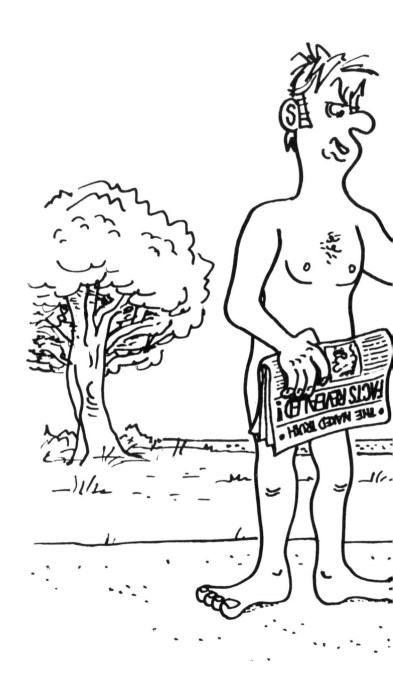

A midget was thrown out of a nudist camp for sticking his nose in other people's business.

A corporate executive was constantly pinching his receptionist at the office. His aim was to harass.

I understand that a sexologist is writing an article about the male reproductive organ after climax; he would like to call it "Withering Heights."

Some women have trouble working for a woman boss. They're used to having a man above them.

A bachelor postman stopped at his girlfriend's house for a quickie before starting his morning rounds. You might say the lady received her male early that morning.

Two sorority girls went away for an intimate ski weekend with their boyfriends. The day they arrived at the ski lodge, they sent a postcard to a sorority sister that read: "There isn't any snow yet, but we are expecting seven or eight inches tonight."

A sixty-year-old man had to give up sex with his wife for a few months because of a prostate operation. However, now he is back in the groove.

Some nurses can make a bed without disturbing the patient; others can make the patient without disturbing the bed.

A college girl does not have to be an English major to know that "to lay" is the object of a proposition.

Many former prostitutes go to work for the IRS. They know all about internal revenue.

A number of men who make it with the ladies soak themselves in an ice-cold bath before going out. They realize that cooler heads will prevail.

During World War II, battles between ships on the high seas and sexual intercourse had much in common. They were both naval encounters with the loss of semen.

I was told that many players on the Pittsburgh Pirates like to go out with women with boyish figures. This preference is not surprising since a pirate's dream has always been a sunken chest.

A dejected man who was afraid of losing his masculinity with age had an affair with a much younger woman to boost his spirits. However, the affair did not help his state of mind. When the woman wanted to make love twice in a row, the man realized he was too depressed. (A number of depressed men believe that making love to an attractive woman will give them a lift.)

A bisexual at a nudist camp could not decide whether he should check out the men or the women. Finally, he left the decision to the flip of a coin—heads or tails.

Gardeners have trouble explaining how the male organ can be fully grown before planted.

A friend of mine used to read his news magazines every week. Now he spends his time reading various men's magazines instead. You might say he has been getting a little behind in his reading.

While I did my best to polish the writing in *Grime and PUNishment,* there is still a lot of raw material in the book. Hopefully, however, the raw material will appeal to laymen (and laywomen) as well as to professional punsters.

X-CITING PUNS

A well-known comedian was bleeped on a late-night talk show when the host asked him what he wanted most in a woman and he replied, "About nine or ten inches."

The director of a porno movie auditioned a young actress to see if she could handle the part.

A woman was complaining to her playboy hairdresser about how difficult it was to take care of her long straight hair. Her hairdresser replied with a smile, "Would you like to be bald?"

My neighbor's wife came home unexpectedly one day and found him in bed with another woman; the man was scared stiff.

A sergeant and two men from his platoon went to a tavern near the base one night. When the sergeant asked an attractive army nurse to join him in a game of pool, the nurse said she would rather play with his privates.

The ideal position for a prostitute on a woman's touch football team would be wide receiver.

A man took out his tailor's daughter and spent a most enjoyable night with her. In the morning he told her that she was the only thing her father ever made that fit him.

Experienced women know that the first thing to come out of the male organ during lovemaking is the wrinkles.

A lawyer and his secretary were at the office late one evening allegedly to organize files and straighten his office. The lawyer's wife happened to stop by the office and found the secretary going through her husband's drawers.

I understand that hookers do not play golf because they cannot keep their balls straight.

A south Florida newspaper wanted to do a story about prostitutes in the Miami–Fort Lauderdale area during the tourist season. A punster editor suggested that a good title for the story might be "The Tail of Two Cities."

Sexologists have learned that American Indians living along the northern Pacific coast often refer to their erections as scrotum poles.

A politician during the recent election allegedly told some staff members that his incumbent opponent should only make love with his wife on top because he's used to screwing up.

I understand that the movie *American Gigolo* is about a working stiff.

Some gigolos will make love to any woman at any time. They're always hard up.

A woman was no longer able to reach sexual climax with her boyfriend. She decided to seduce a good looking man in her office and try him on for sighs.

Most dentists turn out to be great lovers. They're used to drilling cavities.

Supposedly, major league shortstops make great lovers. They're used to going deep in the hole.

A marathon runner, who had been wearing a tight athletic supporter for the past three hours, asked his girlfriend to join him in the bedroom so he could slip into something more comfortable.

A fifteen-year-old virgin alleged that her boyfriend raped her. The authorities charged the boy with breaking and entering.

A couple of successful prostitutes bought a large ranch in Nevada to use as their place of business. Their first customer was a rancher from Texas who told one of the ladies before he left, "Ma'am, you have quite a nice spread here."

Some women do not like attending orgies because they are always surrounded by a bunch of nuts (and after a while, they get tired of screwballs).

A shapely college girl who had not seen her boyfriend all summer threw herself into his arms and said, "Hug me till I break!" Her boyfriend squeezed her until he felt her crack.

There is a special bakery in San Francisco that makes cookies in the shape of the male reproductive organ. They bake their dough in a peter pan, and sell the cookies with doughnuts. (You might say the bakers knead to make women happy.)

A man walked into a porno movie theater wearing nothing but shoes, socks, and a raincoat. When the usherette at the door asked to see his ticket, the man opened his coat and exposed himself. The woman calmly replied, "I asked to see your ticket—not your stub."

An overweight middle-aged woman was physically attracted to a good-looking young guy and thought she could lure him into an affair with her sex appeal. You might describe the woman as a cock-eyed optimist.

Male members of the British government try to avoid involvement with inept female carpenters. They know that one improper screw can cause an entire cabinet to fall apart.

A man from the city drove to a suburban housing development and was shown a ranch model by one of the developer's sexy salesladies. After being alone in the house with the lady for over an hour, the man returned to the developer's office and said, "You have quite a nice lay out here."

Two male vacationers gave up their plans to visit a nude beach after hearing the tour guide say that prolonged exposure to the tropical sun could result in prickly heat.

A photographer's assistant was madly in love with her boss and anxious to get him alone in the dark. One afternoon while her boss was making blow-ups of some of her negatives, she decided to join him in the darkroom and tried to help him enlarge.

Two hookers were once comparing notes and jokingly suggested that they inform the local Health Department about the epidemic of small cox in the area.

A topless dancer who gets men excited with her body might think of her breasts as an erector set.

Men who get drunk on their wedding night end up doing things half-cocked.

It has been said that the reason semen is white and urine is yellow is so that a man will always be able to tell if he's coming or going.

A gynecologist wanted to write a bestseller about oral contraceptives. He thought of using the title *Screw Pills*.

Recently, male strip shows have become very popular. The well-endowed men who perform try to put their best foot forward.

A woman who jumps from one man's bed to another could be considered a pole vaulter.

Even after studying about the male reproductive organ in their sex education classes, a number of high school girls are unable to grasp the subject.

A call girl was hired for a stag poker party to raise the men between hands.

There is a part-time dancer in Las Vegas who makes big money as a call girl when she's not filling in at one end of the chorus line or the other. In other words, some nights she dances on her right leg, other nights she dances on her left leg, and in between she makes a living.

An enterprising lady of the evening could refer to her source of income as "The Chamber of Commerce."

I know a promiscuous woman who often has uncontrollable crying spells. She's constantly bawling.

There is a call girl living near LaGuardia Airport in New York who entertains a number of pilots. Her source of income is often referred to as "The Cockpit."

Most prostitutes put in long hours. They work around the cock.

A superstitious professional golfer once told a sports magazine interviewer that he has his wife rub his balls for luck before a big tournament to help his putting game.

Some female golfers have trouble with the short putts.

A boxing promotor became quite embarrassed when he was talking about one of the women fighters and said, "Boy, you ought to see her box!"

When a male stripper became tired of his profession and was ready to quit, his boss persuaded him to stick it out a little longer.

Since I have now completed
the pun book
that will gross millions,

it's time to BUTT OUT.

APPENDIX

TECHNIQUES FOR PUNSTERS

If the reader has had the endurance to become familiar with the collection of puns in the first part of the book, he is now ready to develop the punning techniques which I believe separate a true artist from a person who can occasionally rattle off a pun when he hears a familiar word. Discussed below are a few basic techniques and a few secondary techniques, which will guide a punster in developing the ability to blend clever puns smoothly into normal conversation.

First of all, and of utmost importance, a punster who is verbally interacting with other people should only use puns that make sense in the context of that interaction. The mere fact that he knows a pun on a word that comes up in the conversation (or which is brought to mind by the situation) does not mean he should use it at that time unless it reasonably fits in with what is being discussed (or what is happening). A punster should strive to make his puns with a perfectly straight face, in a normal tone of voice, so that they are consistent with the rest of the conversation. When a pun is told in this manner, it is not unusual for at least one person in the group not to know what hit him until someone groans it to his attention. (If no one in the group catches the pun, be sure to stop the conversation, smile, and tell everyone what a great play on words they just missed!)

The following are some illustrations of the first technique from my personal experiences. One night during my college days I was at a restaurant in St. Louis with some friends. We finished our main course, and I asked the waitress for the dessert menu. She replied that the only dessert left that night was rice pudding. I instantaneously responded in a disbelieving tone of voice, "You're putting me on."

A couple of years ago at my old law firm I went to see the bookkeeper about getting reimbursed for some cab fares and other business expenses I had paid for out of my own money. She took out a pad of petty cash slips and had me fill out a couple. When I finished, she said, "Why don't you keep the rest of this pad for future use," to which I replied, "Great! I've always wanted a pad of my own."

Recently, I was in Kansas City on behalf of one of my clients, trying to arrange new mortgage financing for a small shopping center. While driving down a major commercial highway, one of the mortgage bankers I was with said, "Look at all the doughnut shops that are going out of business," to which I immediately replied, "Apparently, they're running out of dough." (For some reason it took an unusually long time to get a loan for that particular shopping center.)

Finally, during the last football season I was very much involved in watching the playoff games on television while my wife was wrapping Christmas gifts. She commented that she needed some ribbon for the gifts, and I promised to go out and get some at the end of the game, in about a half hour. After over an hour had passed, and the game was not over, she said something like, "I'm sure glad I have all this ribbon to wrap the presents," to which I shouted, "Quit ribbing me!"

On all of the above occasions I came up with puns that made sense in light of the remarks directed at me, and which were logical continuations of the ongoing conversations. The puns made in these situations should be contrasted with the following puns which were made by other persons in my presence: "I can't bear the thought" (by a bear exhibit at the local zoo), "That's a lot of bull" (upon seeing a bull from a car on a country road), and "Something fishy is going on here" (upon catching a fish on a Wisconsin lake). When the above puns were made, the amateur punsters involved were merely reciting puns on easily-punable words without regard to the context of the situation; the puns were not meaningful in light of what was happening at the time, nor were they a response to something said or done by another person. An accomplished punster would not have impugned his honor with those puns.

My second technique, which potentially could be the most useful and productive, is utilized in situations where a punster thinks of or is reminded of a good pun he would like to make, but feels he cannot smoothly fit it into the ongoing conversation. In these situations a punster should create tangential conversation or concoct a plausible story that will enable him to make his pun effectively. The created conversation should flow smoothly from and be a reasonably logical extension of the ongoing conversation, and again, should be done in normal tone of voice with a perfectly straight face.

A couple of examples will help illustrate this technique. Some time ago there was a popular discount department store chain in the Chicagoland area called "Shopper's World." One time I was involved in a conversation in which someone was discussing the unpleasantness of her last visit to the dentist. I subsequently went off on a tangent that went something like this: "Speaking of dentists, I just read in the paper yesterday that they are planning to open a huge dental office on the Near North Side with chairs for twenty-five dentists. I think they intend to call the office Chopper's World."

On another occasion, I was with a group of people who were talking about their respective vacations in Europe. When it was my turn, I made up the following story: "Of all the countries in Europe, I had the best time in Finland. That's probably because I speak the language." Someone in the group then said, "You speak Finnish?" I replied, "That's right. However, I must admit that my Finnish isn't too good; but, neither is my beginning."

In both of the above situations I manipulated and altered the direction of the conversation to give myself the opportunity to slip in one of my favorite puns. My audience was not aware that my stories were complete fabrications until I lowered the boom on them. It takes years of dedicated practice to be convincing in setting up a pun in this manner without letting people know that you are not for real.

A variation on my second technique, which has given me a great deal of mileage, is picking up a newspaper or magazine and pretending to read (or summarize) some fictitious event. One time at my in-laws' house I picked up the Sunday paper, pretended to be looking at a specific news account, and said the following: "Did you see this article about the terrorists in Nicaragua?" (My in-laws indicated they had not.) "They tried to kill one of their political opponents, a matador, by planting a bomb in the stomach of one of the bulls in the ring. The whole situation is becoming abominable." (My in-laws subsequently told my wife and me that it was time for them to retire for the night.)

The third basic technique is often invoked when a punster really has to stretch the words in his pun or when the pun he plans to use is a little on the obvious side. Also, this technique can be used when the punster is not sure whether or not he has already perpetrated the pun he has in mind on the people he is with. In all these circumstances, the thing to do is to make the pun by blaming it on someone else.

I have three favorite ways of putting the blame on someone else, which once again can best be illustrated by a few examples. If the subject of Moors comes up in a discussion of history or culture, you might look at the person you're talking to at an appropriate point in the conversation and say with an acknowledging nod of the head, "I know what you're thinking: the Moor the merrier." Alternately, if you happened to be discussing great artistic painters, you might turn to someone with a grimacing look at some opportune moment and accusingly say, "You're probably going to say something like 'Easel come, easel go.'" As another possibility, when the time is right and you are talking about oil with the ideal prospective victim, you can simply say with a look of anguish, "I know. The oily bird gets the worm."

In essence, the third technique is a useful device for the times a punster is a little embarrassed or inhibited about making a particular pun, and a suitable scapegoat is present. In addition, this technique affords one the unique opportunity of being a punster at the same time he is pretending to react like one of the unfortunate victims.

It should be pointed out at this time that there are occasions when the people you are with really do inadvertently make puns. As the enlightened punster, you have the option of either pointing out and complimenting the person on his pun, or letting him know about it with a look and words of anguish, depending on who the unenlightened punster is and the circumstances involved. I recall one particular lecture in my commercial law class at Northwestern University when our professor was discussing a particular case dealing with a swimming pool company. During the discussion, the professor made comments about how the business had "liquidity" problems that eventually forced the owner "to go under," and when the bank that had loaned him money took over, they were anxious to "wash their hands of the business." Considering who was involved and the circumstances, I definitely felt it was in my best interests to compliment the professor on his subtle punmanship.

When the circumstances that would occasion the use of my third technique exist, but it might be difficult or awkward to imply that a particular pun is on someone else's mind, a punster should use my fourth basic technique. The fourth technique is actually a tactful way of coping with the moments of weakness that every punster occasionally has when he feels that he absolutely has to make a certain pun or his mind will not be at ease. If you are the punster when these circumstances occur, the following approach should be taken. At some appropriate point in the conversation, you should make your pun in a very deliberate manner by giving the impression that everyone knows the pun should be said, and it might as well be you who gets the job done. For instance, if the subject again happens to be oil (and assuming you have the courage), you could use expressions like, "You know the old saying—'Oil's fair in love and war,' " or, "You know what they always say—'Oil's well that ends well.' " It should be pointed out, however, that even when this technique and the third one are used, the puns must be reasonably consistent with the context of the conversation and situation, lest the punster lower himself to the level of a mere amateur.

Initially, a punster is likely to use the basic techniques discussed above with adaptable puns he has absorbed and stored in his mind for future reference. Eventually, however, he should start to think like a veteran punster and develop the ability to create new puns spontaneously while involved in ordinary conversation.

In addition to my basic techniques, there are a few secondary techniques which can be used by a person who has already started to think like a seasoned punster and whose ears are attuned to hearing punable words. The secondary techniques are more limited in applicability because their use is more dependent on the specific words of others. Nevertheless, these methods of punning have been used most effectively by some well-known people in the world of comedy, and can offer a talented punster additional excellent ways of PUNishing his victims.

There are occasions when someone will say a word that reminds you of a similar-sounding word. In these situations the punster can pretend that he did not hear what the person said, and inquire whether the person said the word the punster is thinking of. A couple of examples again will best illustrate this technique.

A number of years ago my younger brother Marc came home from a barber shop in Winnetka, Illinois, and my grandfather Jake said to him, "Say, that's a nice haircut. Where did you get it?" My brother replied, "At Smales," to which my grandfather responded, "What! You say it smells?"

There was also the time at one of my summer jobs during college when my supervisor and I were discussing a cost-benefit study we were planning to make for a new highway project. My supervisor said something like, "I have very distinct ideas about how to structure this study," to which I quickly responded, "You say your ideas stink?" (It so happens that I was not rehired by that company the following summer.)

If you are to use this type of punning, the people you are with must cooperate by saying the right words;

also you must have sharp ears and enough punning experience to recognize special words which could spontaneously be turned into questioning puns. (Groucho Marx made extremely humorous use of this method of punning on his *You Bet Your Life* show.)

Closely related to the above technique are the corollary techniques of responding to a punable word said by another person by knowingly continuing the conversation in a direction not intended by the victim (until you pretend to acknowledge your misunderstanding at some point), or by physically reacting to what is said in a manner not anticipated by the victim. Again, a few personal experiences can best demonstrate what I have in mind.

A few years ago, I was shopping for some furniture for my apartment with my girlfriend. At one store, I was talking to a salesman about end tables. The salesman looked at one particular table, which was situated next to my girlfriend, and said, "There's a real beauty. Just look at those legs." I continued to look in the direction of the table and my girlfriend and said something like this, "Yes, those are nice legs. And look at the rest of that body, and those sexy eyes." I slowly turned toward the salesman's puzzled face, hesitated, and then said with a look of sudden enlightenment, "Oh! You mean the table! I thought you meant the young lady." The salesman managed to fake a faint smile and a slight laugh, and politely suggested that I look around the store on my own for a while.

More recently, when I first started working for a law firm, a secretary in the firm and I had a discussion about the work habits of the various lawyers in the office. At one point in the discussion she was talking about how sloppy and disorganized the senior partner's office was, referring to the ever-present foot-high layer of papers on his desk. She subsequently asked me if I kept my drawers neat, to which I replied, "Oh, yes. My wife irons and folds every pair." After hearing her snicker a few seconds later, I pretended to see the light by saying, "Oh you mean my desk drawers. Yes, they're pretty neat." (Bob Cummings made extensive use of this type of humor on his *Love That Bob* show.)

Turning to the second variation, I recall the time a number of months ago when my wife and I were having dinner at a well-known restaurant in Chicago. My wife had ordered trout and I had ordered roast duck. The waiter brought out my wife's dinner and a short time later the captain came out of the kitchen with my roast duck. He approached our table and said in a questioning tone, "Duck?" I instantly ducked my head beneath the table (with my arm over my head), to the total bafflement of the captain, the embarrassment of my wife, and the amusement of the couple at the next table. After the captain stood in silence for a few seconds, my wife said to him, "Yes, he ordered duck," at which point the man put my dinner down with a slight, forced smile and left. It so happened that upon leaving the restaurant, instead of hearing the usual "Good night, please come again," all we heard was "Good night." (The Marx Brothers made excellent use of this form of punmanship in their many movies.)

As a final example of the above two corollary techniques I recall a very recent incident which demonstrates how the two methods of punning can be combined effectively. My wife and I went to a restaurant in a nearby suburb with my cousin Harley. As we walked in the door, the hostess came up to greet us and said to my cousin,

"Check your coat?" Harley immediately proceeded to examine every inch of his coat from top to bottom, then turned to the bewildered hostess and said, "Looks all right to me." (The great Mel Brooks has hilariously combined the two techniques—and used each separately—in his recent movies and personal interviews.)

As with the mishearing technique initially discussed, the misunderstanding and physical reaction techniques require the victim to provide the punster with the right words to play off, and the punster must be able to react spontaneously. These two methods of punning are especially suited to those readers with a flair for the dramatic. . . .

When the reader has thoroughly familiarized himself with a number of the puns in the first part of the book and understands the punning techniques outlined above, he is ready to be unleashed upon the public. Hopefully, the categorical collection and the suggested techniques will serve as a training manual until the art becomes second nature. . . .

Fellow punsters are invited to submit their best puns (including illustrated puns) to: Harvey C. Gordon

> c/o The Punster's Press
> P.O. Box 405
> Glenview, Illinois 60025

Submission of any material shall constitute permission for use by Harvey C. Gordon of the submitted material in any future publication or in any other manner determined by him.

If you laughed your way through *Grime and PUNishment,* you'll find even more PUNishment waiting for you in:

PUNishment
The Art of Punning
or
How to Lose Friends and Agonize People

In *PUNishment,* Harvey C. Gordon emphasizes that "what makes punning an art is the ability to blend puns smoothly into normal conversation and the ability to create clever puns spontaneously in appropriate situations."

　PUNishment uniquely combines a collection of over 400 puns with techniques for punning in everyday conversation. The collection of puns is categorized by subject matter and includes special multilingual puns. The punning techniques, if mastered, will separate the true artist from the mere amateur and provide the ability to lose friends and agonize people.

　Whether used as a training manual by aspiring punsters or enjoyed exclusively as a book of humor, PUNishment *has unlimited potential for making you and your friends laugh.*

A large-format quality paperback
V97263-0.......................... $2.95